Mourning a Stranger

Poems by Niara Perry

Mourning a Stranger

Published by Niara Perry

To request permission, contact the publisher at niara272@gmail.com or www.niaraperry.com.

First paperback edition August 2021

ISBN: 978-0-578-93535-5

Edited by Victoria Muzyk and Letetia Coleman
Cover photo and Greed photo by Devon Watts
Grief photo by Kashara Johnson
Growth photo by Brianna Stumpf

Printed by Ingram Content Group LLC

To those who held me, who bathed me in the light as I mourned strangers and my own innocence—thank you. It is only with my heart so full that there was the overflow to pour into this book.

To anyone who called those strangers family, friend, or even a familiar face, may your grief settle into something resembling peace.

To the strangers I've mourned, you deserved so much more than a protest or a verdict. You deserved old age and the freedom of the benefit of the doubt.

When the world is on fire,
maybe the flames have a better plan.

Contents

I Am Here..11

I. Grief..13

II. Greed..31

III. Growth..45

I Am Here

Today has been hard
Yesterday was draining
Last week was difficult

I am tired
I am scared
I am sad

But I am here

I. Grief

Empath's Guide to Mourning a Stranger

Step one: clean
Tidy every corner until you've found where to put the
intruding thoughts
It won't work
You'll still be reeling with confusion
But you'll still try

Scrub every surface in sight
If you wash away the dirt
Maybe today's lies will go with it
There will be more tomorrow
But tonight you can calm your allergies
Stop the welling of your eyes
The crack in your voice
The nausea of digesting another trauma

Step two: cry
You'll first try to chase your racing thoughts
Want to catch one before you sob
But words aren't necessary to explain the tears
You two are already well acquainted

So cry until you're numb
And you forget that he looked like your friend
Your family
Yourself

That anyone can call themselves Judge Nelson
When they're death sentencing a Black man
Can have the victors back their ruling

Step three: write
Write to fill the very space that you occupy
Leave a literary fossil as proof
That you aren't a practice target
That you won't birth a practice target
That even on your lowest days
You still reach the threshold for humanity

Tulsa

YouTube taught me what really happened in Tulsa
If it was ever whispered in a classroom
White guilt was loud enough to drown it out

How to tell a child of murders on a postcard?
Of lost lives framed in triumph
Of hatred so arbitrary
And jealousy so deep
That they weave tales of "deserved" massacre

But that's the way it's always been
Murders molded into achievements
And films
And fond memories floating in an executioner's head
All while the persecuted are forced to forget
Left with only the stories of family lost to unmarked
graves

We label murders "true crime"
Ponder disappearances as mysteries
We hide massacres with silence
Decide the wound isn't painful if we ignore it
Pretend it won't fester under a band-aid half its size

D.I.S.P.O.S.A.B.L.E.

Decades of begging for the simplicity of a trial
"I can't breathe" *
"Stop shooting" **
"Please don't let me die" ***
Over and over the same sentiments
Simple statements
Achievable requests
Belittled experiences
Left for dead
Each of us wonder who's next

Last words of:

*Eric Garner

**Michael Brown

***Kimani Gray

Strangers

I'm still not sure of the criteria for a "good minority"
Uncertain how to show on sight
That my life is worth living

The depths of me don't radiate from my melanin
My story can't shine through a driver's side window
Just like their intentions aren't labeled for my safety
No green light for allies
Or red to warn of misplaced anger

Instead, we are strangers
Colliding with infinite possibilities
So I move slow for my own sake
Hope their assumptions are unassuming
And wonder how much time they'll give me to speak

(Google) Searches

"Guided meditation"
"Guided meditation for poc"
"Guided meditation for poc needing a moment to not remember
That this society was not made for them"

When your existence has been labeled niche
But your culture allocated for consumption
You learn that "wellness" does not extend to your neighborhood

You realize quickly that the foundation laid by your ancestors
Is now stockpiled in one mansion
Where the paintings are all one style
And the furniture holds one size

I've looked to the forest
For a space to build again
To hang paintings that look like we do
And to house chairs with open arms

I know that it's out there
That some place is waiting to be called home
So I continue hiking
Always searching

"Guided meditation for wanderer wondering where to call home"

Open Wounds

I regret to inform you
That there is no shortcut for allyship
No script to memorize
No handbook to purchase

If there were
I'd hand them out for free
Visit every classroom
And read it to the children myself

I regret to inform you
There is no single apology big enough to fill the
centuries without one
No amount of small "sorries" stacked tall enough
To block the past from sight

There is only effort
Only sincerity
Only the search for discomfort
And the quiet to hear its wisdom
To face its ugly truths

You'll never know how to bleed my blood
But I'll still expect you to try
Still expect you to witness
To speak
To heal

Your fears—
Draped in a half-assed savior complex
Flaunting a crown of anger—
They cling to you
With the fervor of a child
Crashing through a dark hall
Certain that the monster is not far behind

Unhealed and unchecked
You leak toxic
Seep infection
Bleed out society
Until the humanity fades from its eyes

How long until you close the wound?

Am I Not Human?

I've sure convinced myself I am
Sure look a fool
Flaunting around in human wear
With the audacity to make myself an identity
Form myself a community

When I catch myself in the mirror
I see a smile reminiscent of the blooming spring
I see the galaxies that swirl behind my eyes
And intricacies as deep as yours

So imagine my confusion
At your efforts for extermination
Like I'm a different species
A different kind of alive

What creaturehood have you forced upon me?
The kind that may serve under you
But never live nearby
May build you sidewalks
But must walk alongside in mud

If I'm not human, tell me now
Y'all have some fucked-up rules
Stipulations I'd love to renounce

Tell me what you see
Perhaps your wish will come true
I'll shed this humanity you've deemed a facade

And escape your dark boxes too

I'll gain back the vitality choked out of me
Oxygen swelling every muscle and cell
And finally the true monster you've created will soar

Are you ready?

Candles

Tonight, I reminisce on warm lights devoured by
capitalist plights
As I did last night
Last week
Last month

A careless blow from the darkness
Fills the air with more grief than oxygen
More smoke than hope
Suddenly the end of night
Feels like nothing more than a far-off star

I'm told that when the moon is setting
And the sun has yet to awaken
The truest darkness of night is revealed
So the light becomes that much sweeter

But what if dawn rises over a world still burning?
Or a world too depleted to burn
With only misshapen wax and blackened wicks
To serve as memorials of the fire
Only the stagnant familiarity of night
In which to search for survival

Luxury

Luxury: noun
"The state of great comfort and extravagant living"
Think Porsche
Think jet planes
Think comfort at the sight of police
Think childhood of ignorance or carefree unawareness

Luxury: noun
The freedom that comes with innocent until proven
guilty
Instead of guilty until dead
Until buried
Until forgotten in the tides of news

Too many times I've wondered
Which photo would they use if it were my body
Were my father's body
Strewn across the street
What story would they tell to make their murder a
"mistake"

I've worried since age five
Over the smallest actions of my cousins
But my mind never lingers on those of my lightest
friends

That little girl
Aged tenfold by the color of her skin
Couldn't label her worry

Hadn't recognized its dynamics
Didn't know to call it "understanding"

When was innocence deemed a luxury?
Whiteness granted its fragility?
How did we decide which underdeveloped frontal lobes
Are protected by the label of "children"

Welcome to the Afterlife

Welcome to the afterlife
Checking in?
So here's your last memory
Here's all the sounds,
The smells,
The weight of four men pressed into your spine
Each heavy with their own careless racism

Do you want to remember your last breath?
It left a plea for air still resting on your tongue
Left your gasps still ringing in your ears

Sorry to tell you
But on the rock where you made home
Your name hasn't proven enough
Your story isn't enough
Your murder is a movie for the masses
But still it's not enough

They keep ignoring
That you were person
That you were loved
That you were victim

Self-Appointed

Nine point five minutes
Five hundred sixty-nine seconds
Five hundred sixty-nine opportunities to change course
Chances to remember his humanity

But how many seconds did you take to remember how
you'd live on
With blood on your knees
Gasps in your ears
The weight of weeping angry families hanging from
your shoulders

Five hundred sixty-nine times
You deemed yourself Set*
A self-appointed Grim Reaper

Even Hades** never stole a soul for his kingdom
Only welcomed in the new arrivals
Yet here you are
Claiming more power than even kin of Zeus

*Egyptian god of violence, chaos, and storms

**Greek god of the underworld

Home

Where do you go
When they've claimed your home as a battleground?
When they label their misjudgement as your
shortcoming

Dusk to dawn curfews
"For your own protection" they claim
But our homes were written into the story
Included in a war somehow framed as our doing

So where do we go to exist?
What space will you let us call home?

II. Greed

Rotting History

The odor of history rotting
Of it aging in the backyard
Is hidden behind the sweet scent of magnolia
But still, it has crept so close to the house
And settled so irreversibly in our nostrils
That we just say it "smells like home"

Only a proper inspection
A detailed cleaning of each leaf and bitter crop
Every root from which it rises
Can clear the stench

Each seed sprouted, branch reaching, and flower
bloomed
Pulls its nutrients from soil hand mixed by parasites
The same ones that come to suck it dry

Let's not forget where "white" was first deemed a person
Where slavery was first given a color
Where Terrorism rose to be called Patriotism

You cover your nose with fabric woven of lies:
"It's so far in the past"
"It's time to move on"
As if time is synonymous with progress
As if "stagnant" isn't a word
As if the earth on which we stand wasn't fertilized with
blood that did not wish to be shed

You cannot call it history when it is not the past
When it rings out in gunshots and harassing screams
When it's still so close,
That's not history
That's a vine so overgrown
You mistake it for the house on which it creeps

Discomfort

Walk towards the creature
Offer her a hand to smell
An ear that listens
Approach her with care
And with humility

Show her that you
Conductor of your own conscience
Master of your own reaction
Are more than a puppet to fear

Stay with discomfort
Study her slightest moves
Understand the parent from which she spawned
Until you hold her dear as the elders

It's a slow process, the introduction
One of patience and love
And it's a necessary process
Life-saving even to those atop the hill

But discomfort left unapproached and unengaged?
Let her forget your face and fragrance?
That's when she growls
And lunges before you notice

Lesson One

America's errors can be traced
In the whip marks of its slaves
The ones that built it
That died for it
The ones that never knew their own home for it

Don't tell me it isn't true
When I traded familiar faces for fully-funded education
Used outside expectations for flotation
And clung so tight
That I found the ocean floor when they hardened to anvils

I didn't learn self-love where I learned to read
Those were lessons for home
Were for Mama to teach

Unit one: self-love
Unit two: self-celebration
Unit three: dark skin is not the same as darkness

All these lessons, taught within walls where I took nightly solace
All these lessons, but no quiz necessary
Mama knew the world would test me plenty

The Tended

Time heals any wound
So long as it is tended to
Only when infection is cleaned away
And the wound ceases to be inflicted

Time is strong
But time lifts no pain alone
It pulls only its own share
Calling on grief, love, and growth to pull the rest

We haven't grieved a full cycle
Haven't approached a new stage
To see how we may heal
Without being given ten new reasons to grieve
To run back into the fields
Frantic to tend to the freshly dropped body

Resting in Someone Else's Bed

The bed you made isn't very comfortable
But you wouldn't know that
Since you don't like to lie in it
Don't like to look at it
Don't like to remember that it's there

What it must feel like
To lie in a bed built, polished, and tucked
By hands other than your own
It's no wonder you ignore your own creation
It collapses in on its sleepers
Leaves wounds and cuts on those simply looking for
peace

Do you even remember your death trap in the corner?
Do you understand why we're so tired?
That atrocity is where we get our semblance of rest

Do you even hear our cries?
Us begging to remove the sharp edges
Or have you found the earplugs?
The nicely fabricated bedtime story
Have you drifted off to your restful night?
Cuddling close to your dreams of self-sufficiency and a
clean conscience

Protesting

The idea of a protest gone "bad" never scared me
I understand the dangers
Know the public can get a little rowdy
But I also understand the dangers of leaving the house
Of driving
Of occupying space

Some things I will not avoid

What does scare me
What has birthed a nervous habit of smiling for my
safety
Is enforcers reinforced with weapons and legislation
Instead of training and information

Protesters will let me walk away
They don't mind if I leave
But enforcers will remind me
That my survival is a protest
That to them I have no worth
And they can beat it into me until I agree

Father's Love

Have you ever been scared?
Like feet frozen
Heart racing
Trapped in a moment you didn't ask for

Then, clear as the sirens in your ears
Your father's voice breaks through the numbness:

"Inside now!"
"Away from the door!"
"Down from the window!"

In those few seconds
You realize he's been preparing this drill
These roadmaps to your safety
From the moment he heard your first cry

He knew as he first felt your weight
As he welcomed you to his eternal love and protection,
That a day would come to act as your shield
As your movement when you could not
Not because of your actions
Or consequence of your mistakes
But simply because you breathed the air of America

A Pleasant Surprise

If I tell you that your support has been a pleasant
surprise
That I feel more at ease now in your presence
Please don't ask why I never voiced my discomfort
before

I have survived
And am trained
From my first step out of the house and into the world
Not to make anyone uncomfortable
Not to make too big a scene
Trained to play by their rules
So that with each sunset, I can rest in my own bed
So that I can find a way to dream and laugh somewhere
between the trauma

These are the only survival tactics I've known
And it's your system that showed me how to use them
So now it's your words that must first break the silence

Blinders

I do not recommend using caucacity as blinders
Sure, they'll keep your focus pointed directly ahead
But ahead isn't the worst part
The hardest part is the burning right beside you
The screams of those in pain

The flames may not yet lap at your feet
But they're not far from it
Fueled by the trash you left along your path
The byproduct of your plush ride

You've soiled the streets
You're burning the village
Stop trotting like it's not your concern
As if distance can leave you untouched

But remember as you plan your own escape
That your town thrives on the pillaging of ours
So tell me how you'll fuel your village
Once ours is only ashes

Allies?

My footing still trembles along this line
The one between welcomed guidance down a new road
And the droning bark of a sheepdog long after the
shepherd has quit

Allyship shouldn't need my congratulations
My kind words
Yet I can't unknow how I need allyship
And how it don't need me

Without allies, I'm just another voice in the field
Too far from Master's house for my screams to haunt his
dreams
Without allies, my brothers and sisters
Mothers and fathers
Are left alone to tend each other's wounds
Left to attend our own funerals
And calm our own tears

But if allies tire
If they've decided to take a seat
What do they lose?
The rush of a "job well done"
For helping out the poor Negroes?

Told

The world has told me "no"
Has told me "change"
Has set my aim on what I will never be

The world said I should come in
As it watched the locked door
Tremble under my pounding fists
"Just use the key!"
It hollered with frustration
Ignoring the cool metal object already in its grasp

III. Growth

Swallowed Screams

I can feel inside me
All the screams swallowed by those before me
And the tears held behind lash lines
All the lives left deconstructed
In the wake of cruelty unmatched

They all sit
Passed through generations
Inextricably intertwined with my every cell
I'm trying to fully digest them this go-round

What do I do with 400 years of unheard screams?
Of unshed tears?
Of defenseless hands?

How to show the world who I am
When it doesn't look at my ancestors
Won't remember their hell
Can't acknowledge my DNA

I feel the tears inside of me
And refuse to let them go unshed
I feel the screams within me
And have decided to no longer stifle them

My pain will be heard
My joy will be celebrated
My existence, every particle of it, will be seen

Family Heirloom

In the wake of a restless night
I spiral to consciousness
Fall up the rabbit hole
Landing back on the banks of a world
More confusing than the dreams I left behind
Ringing in my head is only the whisper of lessons
learned

"Remember yourself
What you need and what you've seen
Remember what you've earned
And what does not need earning
Guard this with strong love
With soothing compassion and grace"

In a world set to decide who you are
Where trauma begets trauma
Your most powerful treasure
And sharpest skill
Is to live so deeply
To root so purposefully
That they cannot rip you from where you stand

Enough

All my years
I've tried to fit
Tried to meet all the standards
Exceed all the standards

And yet, all my years, I haven't felt
Enough
Thought I couldn't do
Enough
Just wanted to be
Enough
Believed that I am the reason that I wasn't

But I've burnt out
And I'm frustrated with using each second to prove
myself
As if my worth only shows in the moments I'm of use

I ache from a lifetime of squeezing into tight spaces
With tight smiles
And careful words
Lugging thick filters

For so long, I'd assumed the pressure of these walls was
how it felt to have skin
When I'd try to leave their confines
When I'd force a step beyond
Fear sank its claws deeper
Told me it's dangerous to leave your own skin

Yet I persist, a new form of exhaustion arising
A new type of lesson seeping in
I learn how to scream that I'm valid
That I'm valuable
Without losing my voice

It's time to follow this fuller fatigue
Because I no longer can fit inside those walls
Won't quietly key the door

I'm pounding
I'm breaking
You'll hear me crashing through

I'm valuable
I'm valid
And I'm all I need to be

SBW

Black women aren't born strong
There is no gene passed through generations
Melanin holds no power to fortify the mind

Just after she fully exits the womb
There is one single second
In which she has the chance to breathe
To be a baby and nothing more

But that luxury is short lived
Second two: necessity rushes into play
Second three: survival
And suddenly her fate is sealed

In that moment
She can do nothing more than await the safe embrace of
her mother
Yet she's already destined
Forced to become
Strong Black Woman

Black Girl

Black girl stand tall
Black girl hold strong
Black girl hold head high
Just so she don't drown

Black girl bilingual
Know two worlds
Know their lingo
Black girl find survival
At what cost?

Black girl too much
At Black girl they stare
From Black girl they yank dignity
Call it theirs

Black girl is done
No more asking for permission
Black girl won
Rose
Bloomed

Black girl honor Black girl
Black girl love herself
Rejoice in herself
Black girl feed herself praise

Tall

You look down upon me
Assumed superiority a mere afterthought
But I stand taller than you realize

You stare toward the ground
See only half of my full stature
My full potential

For years, I'd scrunch low
Bring my face down to meet your gaze
But my back is tired
It hurts in unnatural positions
I can no longer feed my self-destruction with your
accommodations

I'd forgotten how free it is to stand so tall
How stable I balance at my full height
How I dance so powerfully when demanding that you
look up

Lighten My Load

I will no longer carry the weight of blame meant for you

For too long, my steps have been burdened with your
mistrust
Yet still I have made it look graceful
Still I have walked to your beat

But no longer will I inflict your pain upon myself
You are free to try
But do it while you look me in the eyes
While you acknowledge my humanity
Do it while you strip away pieces of your own

Never Have I

Never have I wished I wasn't Black
Never have I avoided sun for fear of delving into deeper
shades
Never have I blamed my skin for these struggles

My blame, I assure you, is placed squarely on those who
forgot to love my skin
Who wish to see it pierced
With bullets and knives
Those who look away when it is

Never have I blamed my skin
Because I always knew the truth:
We are beautiful, my skin and I
My hair and I
My big lips, thick hips and I

We are powerful
I see it every time she soaks in rays meant to scorch her
Reflecting them back out with rainbow-speckled grace

So I have never once blamed my melanated skin for
another's jealousy
Just as I'd never blame the stoic elephant
When it falls at the hands of a poacher

To exist is not the crime
To steal joy
To steal dreams

Innocence
Lives
That's the crime
That's the harm that cannot be undone

55

Magic

I love many things about my brown skin
Plenty of times I am caught in awe of her
But my absolute favorite
Is how she glistens in the sun

In childhood, I would stare mesmerized
As she breathed in the stars
Just to transform into a living crystal

I'd move ever so slightly to see her rainbow specks dance
in the light
Turn my shoulder, my hand, my thigh
Into their dance floor

It felt like magic
Yet I knew it was my own skin performing
So, in those moments, I thought that just maybe
I could be magic too

Announcements of the Soul

From our youngest of days
We are taught that our melanin instills a special
responsibility
One to comprehend dynamics
To twist and fit into cubbyholes provided

But more than that, we are taught to contort with a smile
To move like we're relaxed
Like it doesn't crush us day by day

On the contrary, we should make you feel comfortable
Feel bigger
Feel better
How else could the depth of our color be anything but a
threat?
Could the strength of our ancestors be put to rest?

From today on, I release that responsibility
Decide your comfort isn't worth my silence
My injury
My fear

So hear these words:
No part of me is yours
I am the daughter of daughters of daughters
Whose radiance was inexhaustible

No longer will I be moved to such disrespect of them
As to pretend I am not all of the power

The genius
The feminine
The divine that they gifted to me

Today I declare
Not from the rooftop
But from my soul
Whose heights no building could ever reach
That my light will shine as bright as possible
That it's not my concern if the beauty blinds you

Dear Little Black Baby

Dear my lovely Black bundle of joy
Light of my life
Joy of my future
Hear me when I speak this truth:
You are worthy
You are all the things they've tried to tell you you're not

Dear my smiling Black baby
Please don't let that fade
I am fighting to give that smile a path to the front
But know that they'll still aim to snatch it as you go
So hold your head high
Your smile beaming back at the sun
Too far from their grasp to steal

Dear my ambitious Black toddler
Don't let their words and images
Their glares and stares
Define you
Define *you*
Because you are honored to be beautiful Black baby
But only you know what that means

Dear my unique Black child
Don't let them tell you who you are
Or frame you as unloved
Because, little Black baby, even if you're all grown up
We love you like no other
No ifs, ands, or buts

Be

If I had to choose
If I could ask to be everything I wanted to be

I'd be Black
I'd be female
I'd be queer

All over again

A very big thank you to the visual talent that helped bring *Mourning a Stranger* to life:

Cover and Part II Greed

Devon Watts

devonalexwatts@gmail.com

Part I Grief

Kashara Johnson

www.kasharajohnson.com

www.instagram.com/kashara_johnson/

Part III Growth

Brianna Stumpf

www.instagram.com/briannastumpf/

www.ingramcontent.com/pod-product-compliance
Lightning Source LLC
Chambersburg PA
CBHW050000070726
47592CB00019B/1662